Domesticities
for Flute and Piano

Jon Jeffrey Grier

Piano

About the Composer

Jon Jeffrey Grier holds a B. A. from Kalamazoo College, a M. M. in both composition and theory from Western Michigan University, and a D. M. A. from the University of South Carolina. He studied composition with Lawrence Rackley, Ramon Zupko, Jerry Curry, Dick Goodwin, and Sam Douglas. He taught advanced placement music theory and music history at the Greenville Fine Arts Center (a magnet school), where he was three times named Teacher of the Year.

Program Notes

The five pieces that comprise this suite are designed to evoke everyday events and activities, humorous (at least in hindsight!), invigorating, sentimental, or nostalgic. Mundane events in some ways, they comprise the fabric of normal family life and are experiences shared by all of us.

Contents

Performance Suggestions

If the final movement is played as a stand-alone piece, as any or all may be, begin the performance at measure 5 rather than at measure 1. The motif that comprises the third movement is the name of his wife, represented beneath the title of the movement in the full score.

DOMESTICITIES

Jon Jeffrey Grier

I. Where Are My Keys?

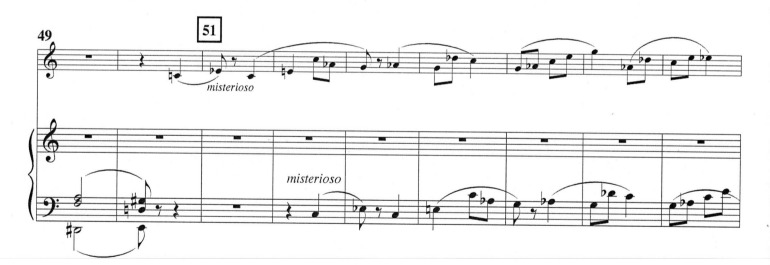

II. A Good Old Dog Goes Out

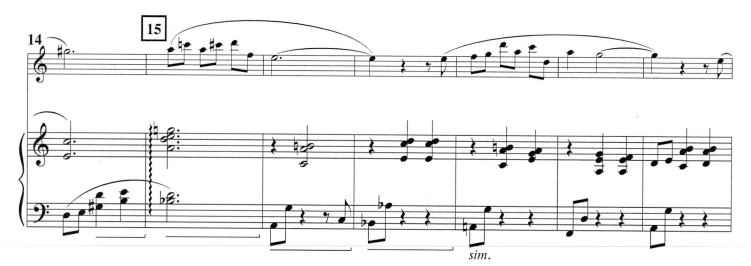

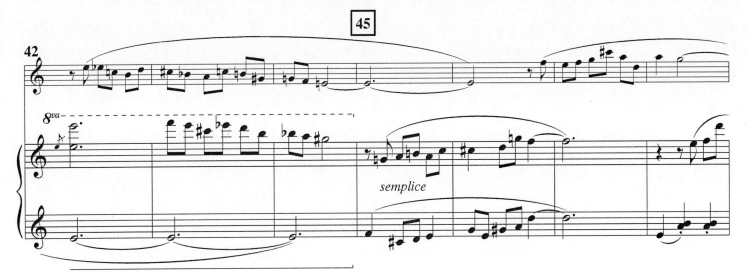

50410012

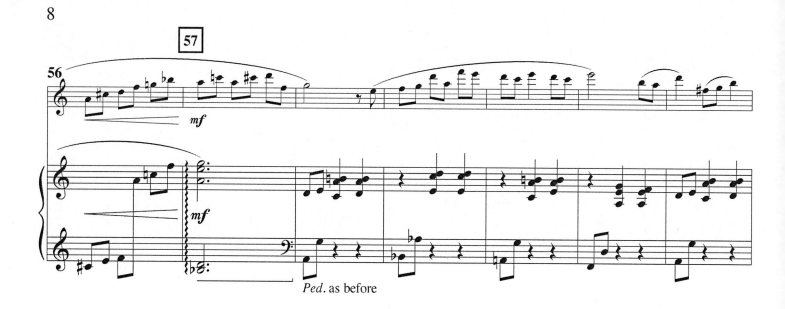

III. Bike Hike

Domesticities
for Flute and Piano

Jon Jeffrey Grier

Flute

About the Composer

Jon Jeffrey Grier holds a B. A. from Kalamazoo College, a M. M. in both composition and theory from Western Michigan University, and a D. M. A. from the University of South Carolina. He studied composition with Lawrence Rackley, Ramon Zupko, Jerry Curry, Dick Goodwin, and Sam Douglas. He taught advanced placement music theory and music history at the Greenville Fine Arts Center (a magnet school), where he was three times named Teacher of the Year.

Program Notes

The five pieces that comprise this suite are designed to evoke everyday events and activities, humorous (at least in hindsight!), invigorating, sentimental, or nostalgic. Mundane events in some ways, they comprise the fabric of normal family life and are experiences shared by all of us.

Performance Suggestions

If the final movement is played as a stand-alone piece, as any or all may be, begin the performance at measure 5 rather than at measure 1. The motif that comprises the third movement is the name of his wife, represented beneath the title of the movement in the full score.

DOMESTICITIES

Jon Jeffrey Grier

I. Where Are My Keys?

50410012

V.S.

Flute

II. A Good Old Dog Goes Out

Flute

III. Bike Hike

Con spirito ♩ = 120

14

27

36

6

Flute

IV. Late, Again

50410012

Flute

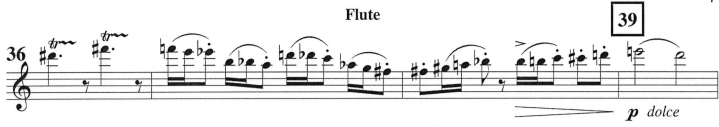

Flute

V. Back Porch Sundown

IV. Late, Again

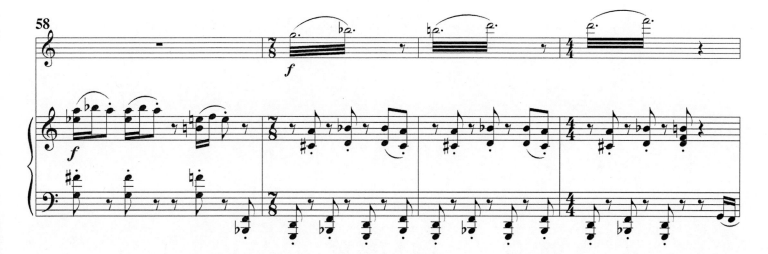

V. Back Porch Sundown

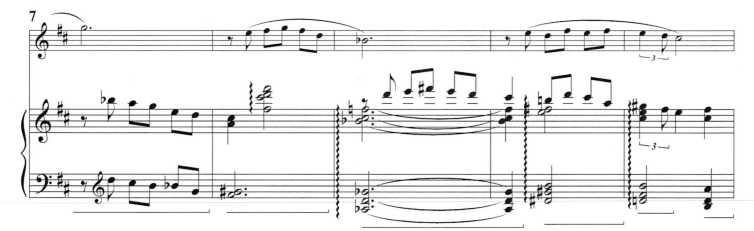

50410012

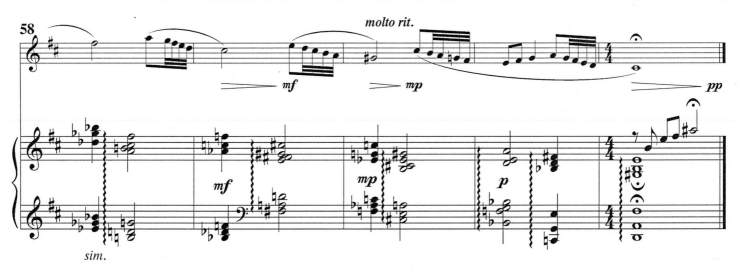

Selected Flute Publications

SOLO, UNACCOMPANIED

FERROUD, PIERRE OCTAVE
M284891   Three Pieces

SOLO WITH PIANO

BUSSER, HENRI
M114291   Petite Suite

M298091   Prelude Et Scherzo

CASELLA, ALFREDO
M266891   Barcarola E Scherzo

M371291   Sicilienne and Burlesque

CHAMINADE, CECILE
M114791   Air De Ballet, Op. 30 and Serenade Aux Etoiles, Op. 142

W112691   Concertino, Op.107

DEBUSSY, CLAUDE
M168591   Clair De Lune

DOPPLER, FRANZ
M384191   Chanson D'amour, Op. 20

M127191   Fantaisie Hungarian

M335491   Fantasy Pastorale Hongroise

GANNE, LOUIS
M127091   Andante Et Scherzo

GAUBERT, PHILIPPE
M186691   Deux Esquisses
"Two Sketches" written by French flautist, Philippe Gaubert. Movements: I. Night on the Plain II. Oriental.

M122791   Nocturne Et Allegro

M218391   Sonata In A

M196191   Two Pieces (Sicilienne/ Madrigal) for Flute and Piano
Two pieces for flute and piano by the French master, Philippe Gaubert, dedicated to flautist Gaston Blanquart and Marie Edme Jules Bucquoy, MD. Titles Included: 1. Sicilienne 2. Madrigal

GERMAN, EDWARD
M330491   Suite
Dedicated to the composer's friend, virtuoso Welsh flautist Frederic Griffith. Movement Titles: 1. Valse Gracieuse 2. Souvenir 3. Gipsy Dance.

GLIERE, REINHOLD
M330691   Two Pieces, Op.35

GLUCK, CHRISTOPH WILLIBALD
W704191   Concerto In G

GOOSSENS, EUGENE
M131291   Three Pictures

GRIFFES, CHARLES TOMLINSON
M282291   Poeme

GROVLEZ, GABRIEL
M152591   Romance And Scherzo

HAHN, REYNALDO
M342491   Two Pieces
This reprint edition contains two pieces for flute and piano by Reynaldo Hahn dedicated to French flautists Louis Fleury and Gaston Blanquart respectively. I. Danse pour use deese (Dance for a goddess) II. L'Enchanteur (The Enchanter)

HARTY, HAMILTON
M292591   In Ireland
Dedicated to British harpist Miriam Timothy, this fantasy is written to evoke the image of two street musicians playing in a Dublin street at dusk.

IBERT, JACQUES
M218491   Aria

KARG-ELERT, SIGFRID
M360191   Symphonic Canzona

MONTI, VITTORIO
M263991   Czardas

MORLACCHI, PIETRO
M395791   Il Pastore Svizzero

MUTHEL, JOHANN GOTTFRIED
M134991   Sonata In D Major

RAVEL, MAURICE
M169091   Pavane Pour Une Infante Defunte (flute/piano)

REINECKE, CARL
M384091   Ballade Op. 288

W100891   Concerto Op. 283

ROSENHAUS, STEVEN
P001791   Rescuing Psyche
Rescuing Psyche for flute and piano was commissioned by the Music Teachers National Association and the NYSTMA and was premiered by flutist Kelly J. Covert and pianist Nathan Hess. Rescuing Psyche takes its inspiration from Greek mythology. Eros, a god, and Psyche, a mortal, are in love, but Aphrodite is jealous. Aphrodite successfully traps the mortal in a coma, but Eros wakes his love by playing a flute. The flute part has some key clicks and flutters but no other extended techniques or special effects are required.

SAINT SAENS, CAMILLE
M207091   Romance, Op. 37

TELEMANN, GEORG PHILLIPP
M198891   Sonata in B minor

VIVALDI, ANTONIO
M201791   Sonata In C, Rv 48

WIDOR, CHARLES-MARIE
M183591   Suite, Op. 34

KEISERSOUTHERNMUSIC.COM

Questions/ comments? info@laurenkeisermusic.com